ASSESSMENT & LEARNING
Pocketbook

By Ian Smith

Cartoons:
Phil Hailstone

Published by:

Teachers' Pocketbooks
Laurel House, Station Approach,
Alresford, Hampshire SO24 9JH, UK
Tel: +44 (0)1962 735573
Fax: +44 (0)1962 733637
E-mail: sales@teacherspocketbooks.co.uk
Website: www.teacherspocketbooks.co.uk

*Teachers' Pocketbooks is an imprint of
Management Pocketbooks Ltd.*

Series Consultant: **Brin Best**.

This edition published 2007.

ISBN 978 1 903776 75 9

British Library Cataloguing-in-Publication
Data – A catalogue record for this book is
available from the British Library.

Design, typesetting and graphics by Efex Ltd.
Printed in UK.

Contents

Introduction

This book is a result of four years spent reflecting on issues around assessment in schools, and working with Scottish teachers to help them take advantage of the national 'Assessment is for Learning' initiative, the Scottish equivalent of Assessment for Learning in England, Wales and Northern Ireland.

My colleagues and I have run hundreds of workshops with thousands of teachers all over the UK. Having worked in education for over 30 years, promoting and supporting changes in classroom methodology, I can say that no other initiative in that time has had such a beneficial impact on classroom practice as 'Assessment for Learning'. Teachers at all levels like it because it is full of practical ideas that work day-in-day-out in classrooms.

I like it because it is not just about tips for teachers (though there's nothing wrong with that!). It's also theoretical: the ideas are based on our current understandings about how we learn – what helps us to learn and what can hinder us from learning. Also, I believe it both requires and helps teachers to carve out a defined role for themselves in the classroom: one that involves less spoon-feeding and more helping pupils to take more responsibility for their own learning. It's what I call 'letting go so they can get going'.

Introduction

The greater emphasis on assessment for learning in the UK – and increasingly throughout the world – owes a great deal to the ground-breaking research undertaken by Professors Paul Black and Dylan Wiliam and first published by King's College, London in *Inside the Black Box* (1998) (see page 124). They carried out a survey of research into the effects of formative* assessment across 24 countries and concluded that it was in great need of development.

Their trawl of the research came up with three main findings:

- Effective formative assessment raises standards, especially for so-called low attainers

- The everyday practice of assessment in classrooms is beset with problems and shortcomings

- There is lots of evidence of practical ways to improve formative assessment

*See pages 8-18

Introduction

Black and Wiliam, with colleagues from King's College, took their findings to practising teachers, encouraging and helping them to apply the ideas they felt would work for them in their classrooms.

Their initial research encouraged many others, including ourselves, to do the same and from that work has come a wide range of practical strategies and techniques for improving assessment for learning across subject areas and age groups. Those strategies and techniques are the main subject of this book.

We begin, however, by getting behind the jargon of assessment, defining what is meant by assessment *of* learning and assessment *for* learning and highlighting some of the issues that Black and Wiliam's research threw up about the negative effects the present system of assessment in UK schools can have on the attitudes and motivation of students and teachers and, therefore, on the quality of learning and teaching in classrooms.

Assessment and Learning ◀

 Learning Intentions and Success Criteria

 Quality Interaction

 Verbal Feedback

 Written Feedback

 Assessment by Pupils

 Getting Started

 Further Information

Assessment and Learning

Why do we assess?

Assessment plays an essential part in education generally and in learning and teaching particularly. Teachers and schools are expected to assess students' learning for a range of purposes and for a range of audiences.

Assessment primarily carried out to help pupils to learn is usually called **formative assessment** or **assessment *for* learning.**

Assessment which is primarily for other purposes is often called **summative assessment** or **assessment *of* learning.**

Why do we assess?

To monitor national standards	**Evaluative**	**Assessment**
To make teachers, administrators and politicians accountable		**of** Learning
To sort and classify students for university and employers		
To determine what courses students should take in school	**Summative**	
To report on achievement to students themselves and parents		
To support and help students to learn by diagnosing difficulties	**Diagnostic**	**Assessment**
To support and help students to learn by providing feedback	**Formative**	**for** Learning

There's a growing acceptance that education systems throughout the world place too much emphasis on assessment *of* learning and too little emphasis on assessment *for* learning. This book looks at how schools and teachers can redress the balance.

But first let's look at why we need to.

Assessment *'of'* and *'for'* learning

Many people find it difficult to see the difference between summative and formative assessment. After all, the same results or the same evidence can often be used by different people for both purposes.

But the two kinds of assessment are quite different. They involve teachers and pupils asking very different questions about themselves and about what they should do next.

Assessment *of* learning (summative)

Mainly about evaluating performance.

Backward looking. Usually comes at the end of a piece of work.

Key questions:
- *'How good am I at this?'*
- *'Is she working to level B yet?'*
- *'Can he do his six times table?'*

Assessment *for* learning (formative)

Mainly about supporting improvement.

Forward looking. Usually takes place continually as you are learning.

Key questions:
- *'How have I progressed?'*
- *'What difficulties is she still having?'*
- *'What help does he need now?'*

Exams and tests

We cannot run our education system without tests and examinations. But there's increasing support for the view that too much emphasis on summative assessment is not only unwise, it can be destructive.

Much assessment *of* learning leads to an emphasis on **performance** and too often is used simply to **identify failure**. It:

- Provides feedback in the form of grades or marks or levels and encourages comparisons and competition
- Is administered by the teacher and comes at the end of a chunk of learning
- Can lead learners who lack confidence in their ability to opt out or 'retire hurt'

By contrast, assessment *for* learning is constructive because it focuses mainly on **improvement** and is used to **support progress**. It:

- Helps learners to know how well they have learned and provides feedback on how they can do better
- Encourages learners to support and help each other while they are learning
- Builds self-motivation, self-confidence and self-reliance

Why assessment can be damaging

A seminal study of the effects of the two kinds of assessment on classroom learning in over 20 countries was published by King's College in 1998*. It pointed out that an over-emphasis on assessment of learning in schools had had a negative impact on the motivation of both pupils and teachers:

Implications for pupils' motives

When assessment is being used by someone else to **evaluate** your learning, if you lack confidence you are more likely to:	When assessment is being used to help you **improve** your learning, even if you are under-confident you are more likely to:
• Hide what you don't know and find difficult • Always look for the right answer • Focus on your mark or your grade • Want to know your place in the class	• Be honest about what you don't understand • Be open to lots of ideas or answers • Focus on the teacher's comments • Want to know how you have done in comparison to how you did before

*Black P and Wiliam D (1998a) *Assessment and Classroom Learning*. Assessment in Education, Principles, Policy and Practice, 5(1) 7-73

Why assessment can be damaging

Implications for teachers' motives

When assessment is being used by someone else to **evaluate** your teaching, if you lack confidence you are more likely to:	When assessment is being used to help you **improve** your teaching, even if you are under-confident you are more likely to:
• Find the right label for the work, eg 'This is a 'D' '	• Work out how to help a child improve, eg 'How could this become a 'C'?'
• Get your evidence in writing	• Collect lots of informal evidence from questioning, listening and observing
• Test as late as possible - when you are sure they will succeed	• Test half way through a topic to help you identify difficulties early on
• Tell them what is coming up	• Spring a test on them so it is a true test
• Teach to the test	• Teach the topic but respond to children's interests
• Be concerned about how well your class has performed in relation to others or to the national norm	• Be concerned about what difficulties your class has had and how you can use that information to improve your teaching and their learning

Balancing summative and formative assessment

The fact that this pocketbook focuses on developing assessment for learning does not imply that assessment of learning is worthless or necessarily detrimental.

Pupils need to know how well they are doing, as do parents and teachers. Employers, colleges and universities need results from examinations to decide which candidates are likely to be suitable for jobs or courses. Schools and teachers need to be accountable. However, do pupils need to know where they stand **all** the time?

 Do we need to keep pulling the plant up to see if it is growing?

Balancing summative and formative assessment

What educationists and teachers are calling for – and what more and more parents are coming to recognise – is the need for a better balance between the two kinds of assessment. They see that to achieve such a balance we need to do less testing and instead help expand our strategies and techniques for assessing for learning.

That's what the rest of this book is about. So let's start by defining in more detail what assessment for learning looks like in practice.

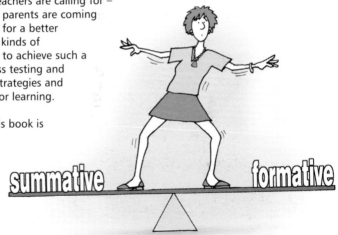

What is assessment for learning?

Paul Black and Dylan Wiliam's 1998 definition of assessment for learning and how it relates to formative assessment has stood the test of time:

In this paper, the term 'assessment' refers to all those activities undertaken by teachers, and their students in assessing themselves, which provide information to be used as feedback to modify the teaching and learning activities in which they are engaged. Such assessment only becomes 'formative assessment' when the evidence is actually used to adapt the teaching work to meet the needs.

Inside the Black Box.

I break assessment for learning down into three key stages:

1. Gathering information about your learners.
2. Analysing and interpreting that information.
3. Using that information to inform your teaching and to help your learners learn for themselves.

Working in the gap

The concept of feedback lies at the heart of assessment for learning. It's about 'working in the gap' between what your learners already know, understand and can do and what they **will** know, be able to understand and do in the future.

The role of the teacher is not to close the gap for their learners but to support them to close the gap for themselves through their own efforts and using techniques that work for them. It is what educationists have called 'mediation' or 'scaffolding' and requires that teachers push some of the responsibility for their learning over to learners themselves.

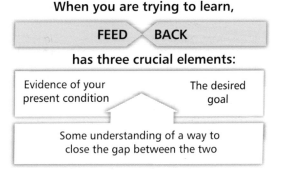

When you are trying to learn,

FEED BACK

has three crucial elements:

Evidence of your present condition

The desired goal

Some understanding of a way to close the gap between the two

Five practical strategies

Assessment for learning focuses mostly on practical teaching techniques.
Five practical strategies make up the following chapters of this book:

1. Sharing learning intentions and success criteria with learners.
2. Engaging in quality dialogue and discussion.
3. Giving immediate high quality verbal feedback.
4. Marking less yet achieving more.
5. Making effective use of peer- and self-assessment.

Learning intentions is a logical place to start. If you and your learners aren't clear about what is to be learned, you don't have a sound basis for class lessons and questioning. Equally, If you're not sure of the success criteria, feedback is unfocused.

Having pupils take more responsibility for their own assessment is where most teachers want to get to. But where you start and in what order you tackle these ideas is, of course, up to you.

Assessment
and Learning

 Learning
Intentions and
Success Criteria

 Quality Interaction

 Verbal Feedback

 Written Feedback

 Assessment
by Pupils

 Getting Started

 Further
Information

Learning
Intentions and
Success Criteria

The big box of secrets

As teachers, when we're under pressure we usually think first about what we are going to teach and second what we are going to ask pupils to do. This is what we tend to share with pupils at the start of a lesson.

We tend to lose sight of what we want pupils to *learn* from undertaking the tasks we set them, ie the **learning intentions**, and how we will know they have been successful, ie the **success criteria**. Even if we're clear about both, we tend not to share them.

Why are we learning this stuff anyway?

What are they looking for? How will I know I've done well?

Young people cannot become more independent learners unless they know what they are expected to learn and how they will know they have been successful.

What do they want me to learn?

This section looks at how to develop accessible learning intentions (pages 22-32) and success criteria (pages 33-42) and how to share them with pupils.

The big box of teachers' secrets

Terminology

All sorts of jargon has been used over the years to describe what I call here 'learning intentions' and 'success criteria'. For instance:

| objectives | outcomes | grade-related criteria | rubrics |

I like the word 'intentions' because it is softer than objectives and outcomes – and it suggests you might not succeed every time! It also suggests that the individual has ownership of the intention rather than it being something handed down from on high, which is where outcomes and objectives come from.

Don't get hung-up on terminology, though: if you are required to use (or prefer to use) other terms, fine. It is, however, a good idea, particularly at primary level, to choose more immediate and accessible constructions to describe the aim of a particular piece of work.

'I am trying to...'

'My next steps are...'

'I want to...'

'I aim to... by...'

Develop your own learning intentions

Identifying the learning intentions for a lesson or series of lessons is usually quite straightforward. You don't have to start from scratch; indeed you can't because you have a given curriculum.

However, rather than accepting what other people give you, you need to make the actual statements you use your own. This will help you to internalize them and communicate them to your learners.

Select a lesson or a series of lessons to work on. To begin with, choose an area you are comfortable with, or you know well, or that pupils find particularly difficult. Gather together what already exists in terms of learning objectives, outcomes and targets from existing curriculum guidelines. Then, go through the steps and use the examples outlined on pages 23-32 to develop learning intentions that make sense to you and your learners.

Nine steps to writing clear learning intentions

1. Use appropriate phrasing and tone.
2. Use child-speak.
3. Emphasise learning rather than doing.
4. Make clear the nature of the learning.
5. For closed skills…
6. For open skills…
7. How will they demonstrate knowledge and understanding?
8. Separate the intention from the context.
9. Make them manageable, accessible and visible.

1. Use appropriate phrasing and tone

How you word an intention affects the willingness of pupils to engage with it. Think about the best phrasing and tone for the children you are working with. Learning intentions can be framed as:

- **Instructions:** *'Use capital letters when writing sentences'*
- **Affirmations:** *'I am going to use capital letters when writing sentences'*
- **Achievements before the event:** *'I can use capital letters when writing sentences'*
- **Goals:** *'To be able to use capital letters when writing sentences'*
- **Learning:** *'I am learning to use capital letters when writing sentences'*
- **Prompts:** *'Remember to use capital letters when writing sentences'*
- **Extra efforts:** *'I will try harder to use capital letters when writing sentences'*

2. Use child-speak

Take time to check that your early efforts produce meaningful learning intentions that pupils can understand. It's challenging at first, but it gets easier with practice.

Even with very young children who are on the verge of learning to read, it's worth using written learning intentions as well as verbalising them and making them visible, eg:

- *'We are learning how to space words when we write'*
- *'We are learning to use a number line to add'*
- *'We are learning to say what we think'*

With older children skill- or knowledge-based learning intentions are easier to translate than concepts. Technical language may cause a problem but learners can generally cope if they are introduced to technical terms early and have had them explained, eg:

- *'We are learning to be able to discuss how a poem uses form'*
- *'We are learning to describe motion from a speed-time graph'*
- *'We are learning to work out the circumference and area of a circle'*

3. Emphasise learning rather than doing

Learning intentions help pupils to focus, not on a task or activity, but on what they will learn from doing it. The words framing the learning intention should reinforce this. So avoid, for example:

- *'We are going to make a poster'*
- *'We are going to be using filter paper to separate solids from liquids'*
- *'We are going to be marking an opponent'*
- *'We are going to read aloud to the group'*

Instead, use words like 'know', 'learning', 'thinking' and 'using' (the senses, skills or tactics). These can all emphasise the focus on learning. For example:

- *'We are learning to know what makes a good poster'*
- *'We are aiming to be able to separate solids and liquids'*
- *'We are learning how to mark an opponent'*
- *'We are aiming to get better at reading with expression in our voice'*

4. Make clear the nature of the learning

One of the real benefits of developing your own learning intentions is that it makes you think about what you really want pupils to learn. Be aware that all areas of the curriculum require a range of different kinds of learning intentions. Ask yourself:

- **What do they need to remember?**
  (recall of facts)
  eg: *'We are learning to remember our multiplication tables'*

- **What do they need to be able to do?**
  (developing skills)
  eg: *'We are learning to be able to add and subtract fractions'*

- **What do they need to realise?**
  (building awareness and understanding)
  eg: *'We are learning to be aware what the 3 in 32 means'*

5. For closed skills...

A closed skill can be described as a skill where there is one right answer or outcome, and one way of getting the right answer or one correct procedure or way of doing something to achieve the right outcome. For example, *'We are learning to:*

- *Work out the area of a triangle*
- *Work out the circumference of a circle*
- *Put capital letters and full stops in the right places in our stories'*

It can be difficult to pitch learning intentions for closed skills at the right level. If they are too small and too easy pupils won't be challenged and the whole system will soon become unmanageable.

On the other hand, if they are too difficult – if pupils don't know the correct procedure or the right answer – they can also be demotivating. Simply framing the intention as an exhortation, eg *'Try to remember capital letters and full stops'*, does not work.

The solution is to focus on the process or procedure involved in getting the right answer or reaching the correct outcome, when writing the success criteria (see page 36).

6. For open skills…

Open skills can be very broad. They are general skills which subsume more specific skills (see previous page), so it is more difficult to evaluate what a good end product is. For example, *'We are learning to…*

- *Write a story*
- *Record an experiment*
- *Present a report'*

Pupils can easily be overloaded if asked to focus too broadly. One way to overcome this is to write more focused 'whole task' learning intentions, eg *'We are learning to…*

- *Write a mystery story, using suspense*
- *Record the results of our experiment accurately and draw conclusions using our scientific knowledge*
- *Present a written, reasoned argument including for and against positions'*

7. How will they demonstrate knowledge and understanding?

When writing learning intentions for knowledge and understanding use action verbs so that pupils are asked to **show** what they know or how they know, or **demonstrate** their understanding in some kind of way. For instance:

Instead of:	Use an action verb:
'I understand why fossil fuels are a finite resource.'	*'I can explain why fossil fuels are a finite resource.'*
'I understand what a miracle is.'	*'I can describe the key features of a miracle.'*
'I understand what it was like to be an evacuee in the Second World War.'	*'I can use evidence to work out what it was like to be an evacuee in the Second World War.'*

8. Separate intention from context

Separating the learning intention from its context is a good way of highlighting the learning as opposed to the activity you're using to achieve the learning. It can also help students to recognise that skills can be applied or transferred to different topics and different situations – something they find particularly difficult. Some examples:

'We are learning about how radio and television receivers work' becomes:

Learning intention: *'We are learning about sound and waves.'*

Context: Radio and television receivers.

'We are learning to paint the sea' becomes:

Learning intention: *'We are learning to use colours to create an effective painting.'*

Context: The sea.

9. Make intentions manageable, accessible and visible

Try to keep to one or two learning intentions per lesson and make them visible and accessible while pupils are working. They can be written in a jotter at the start of a piece of work, for instance, or printed on a bookmark or card that can be moved between different documents.

One school invested in a small whiteboard for every classroom. The teacher wrote the learning intentions on the board. They were wiped off at the end of the lesson and the objective for the next lesson put up.

A maths department used small flipcharts which sat on the teacher's desk. The learning intentions were written up at the start of each lesson and accumulated during a topic.

An early years teacher had a washing line across one corner of her room where she would display in words and pictures the activities children would be involved in during the day, chronologically and with rough timings.

Generate success criteria
with your students

Just as it is important to identify clear learning intentions, so it is to establish clear **success criteria.**

Teachers from early primary to upper secondary argue strongly for the benefits of generating success criteria with pupils. Involving pupils in the process of identifying the criteria they will use to evaluate their response to a specific learning intention helps them to engage with their own learning and take responsibility for it.

It need only be a one-minute brainstorm:
'How will we know if we have achieved this?'
'What will I need to look for to see if you have achieved this?'

For many lessons the success criteria will be contained in one statement. But sometimes it will be worth taking longer to negotiate suitable success criteria with pupils. You can guide them through the process of setting, editing, combining and deleting criteria, enabling them to describe quality in a way that they really can assimilate before embarking on a task designed to expand their learning.

Focus on process

It is important that pupils not only demonstrate their skills, knowledge and understanding but also that they reflect on **how** they got there. Generating success criteria should take teachers and students into discussions of the **processes of learning**: what it is you need to be able to do, know and understand to produce quality. This is particularly important in the area of closed skills:

Don't just refer to the right answer: *'I am looking to see if your work is correct'.*	**Do** give reminders about how to get there: *'I am looking for sentences that begin with capitals and end with full stops'.*
Don't just name an end product: *'I want to see that everyone has made a bowl'.*	**Do** be specific about what the bowl should be like: *'I want to see that you were able to make a bowl that holds water and sits stable on the desk'.*
Don't just make success criteria out of a number of completed or correct answers: *'I am looking for at least four out of five answers correct with working shown'.*	**Do** be clear you want working that shows their strategy: *'I am looking for working that clearly shows me what strategy you have been using to work out the area of 2D shapes'.*

Don't use the same words as the learning intention

By focusing on **the process** in closed skills, teachers can avoid the trap they sometimes fall into of repeating the wording of the learning intention in the success criteria.

For instance, the learning intention might be: *'We are learning to be able to calculate the area of different triangles'*.

It's an easy mistake to make to come up with the following success criterion: *'To be able to calculate the area of different triangles 'accurately' or 'every time' or 'two times out of three'*.

This 'product' criterion simply repeats the learning intention with the addition of an adverb or a scale. While this may be useful for summative assessment purposes, it doesn't help the pupil to learn how to make the calculation, or to put it right for themselves if they have got it wrong. To be effective, the criteria need to focus on the process of making the calculation (see next page).

Devise a checklist

Devising a checklist of steps to reach the end product overcomes the problem of the success criteria simply repeating the learning intention and gives pupils help to carry out the skill. A set of specific criteria which describes the step-by-step process that pupils have to go through to be able to do the calculation accurately really does aid learning:

Learning intention: *'To know how to calculate the area of different triangles.'*

Success criteria: *'Remember to:*
- *Identify and measure the base and height*
- *Multiply the base by the height and divide by two*
- *Record the units in squares'*

This supports the learning and helps learners take responsibility for checking their own or each other's work, working out where they went wrong and putting it right.

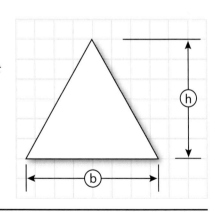

Use a menu of criteria for specific skills

Sometimes a skill is closed in the sense that there is only one right outcome, but you can get to that outcome by different routes or by using the same steps in a different order depending on what works for you as a learner. For example:

If the learning intention is:
'I know what to do when I am stuck at a word.'

The success criteria might be:

- *'I sound out the word'*
- *'I see if it looks like a word I know'*
- *'I read the words around it'*
- *'I look at the picture'*

Reading the word correctly is the one right outcome, but learners might use any combination of strategies from the list or only one that works for them. In that sense it is a **menu** rather than a checklist.

Focus on observable behaviours

Useful success criteria are clear and concrete. It's relatively straightforward to establish these when the outcome is closed, but where tasks are more open-ended, as in writing an essay, say, or practising personal and interpersonal skills, it is more difficult.

One way to overcome this is to focus on 'observable behaviours' by asking: *'What will good look like or sound like in this instance?'* or, *'What will be a fair effort and what will fall short of being acceptable?'*

This can be applied to a product: *'What will a good book report, essay, poster, graph, presentation etc. look like?'*

It can also be applied to a skill: *'What will it look, sound and feel like if your audience appreciates your presentation?'* (Possible criteria: people sitting still, not fidgeting; eye contact with the speaker; no talking; people nodding and smiling; hands up to ask questions; applause at the end.)

Success criteria for open skills in writing

What makes one essay or story better than another is open to debate. The success criteria need to offer a menu of suggestions which can help learners to achieve the broad learning intention. The success criteria for writing a report might be:

- *'Use headings and sub-headings'*
- *'A clear opening'*
- *'Facts to describe the main ideas'*
- *'Facts are in a clear logical order'*
- *'Use suitable words and phrases'*
- *'Have an appropriate conclusion'*

It could be that not all of the suggestions need to be taken up to achieve the learning intention, nor will they need to be used in any particular order. On the other hand, you could include all the suggestions on the checklist and the final product might still not meet the learning intention. With open skills the use of success criteria is always subordinate to the teacher's overall view of the work.

Therefore, as teachers we need to go beyond providing checklists of success criteria and coaching learners to use them. We need to show examples of work that meet the learning intention and discuss and analyse them with pupils to discover why they are successful (see pages 103-104).

Let success criteria emerge in the lesson

It's often assumed that generating success criteria should be done at the start of the lesson and shared up-front with the learning intention. But often (problem solving in Maths for instance) you will want to generate the success criteria *after* the activity has been completed. If your success criteria simply give students the steps they need to take to solve the problem, they will simply work through them mechanically without internalizing or understanding the process.

Equally, many teachers believe that sharing success criteria up-front in more open-ended activities stunts creativity and does not allow pupils the opportunity to learn by making mistakes and going up blind alleys.

In these circumstances the success criteria might be generated at the end of the lesson to help the pupils carry out the task again or to help next year's class undertake the task.

Use characters

You can help pupils to focus on learning intentions and success criteria by using characters they can remember and relate to. This is a favoured approach in primary schools, but secondary teachers also use the idea. It depends very much on your personality and your relationship with your class:

One popular example is **WALT and WILF**. WALT stands for *'We are learning to'*, a child-friendly way of describing a learning intention. WILF stands for *'What I'm looking for'*, the criteria needed to assess success.

Then there's **OLI** the owl. A middle primary teacher encouraged ownership of learning intentions by using OLI (Our Learning Intentions) to emphasise personal involvement. Later she decided she could further their ownership of the idea by putting the class picture up on the wall with *'Our Learning Intentions'* (OLI) underneath it.

And a great favourite, **LOUTS**. A secondary history teacher used the term 'learning outcomes' rather than intentions and called them 'LOUTS'. His pupils were always on the look-out for them, charged to tie them down and bring them into the open.

Don't overuse or overplay

Writing and sharing learning intentions and success criteria with pupils is an essential part of assessment for learning. It helps them:

- Take more responsibility for their own learning and their own assessment
- Learn how to learn

It is the foundation on which the other chapters of this book are built and is something that should be routine, but not overused or overplayed. It should never become mechanical, simply a matter of going through the motions. Sometimes you don't want pupils to know what they are going to learn!

At the very start of lessons you should still focus on describing what children are going to do. Before you share learning intentions with them aim to engage and enthuse them with the activity.

The acid test is: do the learning intentions and the success criteria help pupils to focus on what they are learning and actually help them to learn? If not, they're a waste of time.

Assessment
and Learning

Learning
Intentions and
Success Criteria

Quality Interaction ◄

Verbal Feedback

Written Feedback

Assessment
by Pupils

Getting Started

Further
Information

Quality
Interaction

The importance of high quality interaction

Sharing learning intentions and success criteria with pupils helps them to focus on **what** they are learning and **how** they will know they have learned. This section looks at how, as teachers, we can run lessons that encourage pupils to think and talk about their learning and how we can tune into their thinking.

In a classroom where there is quality interaction, assessment becomes a two-way process: it's not simply about giving feedback to learners but about getting feedback *from* them. That way we can:

- Clarify what learning has taken place
- Identify what difficulties are being experienced
- Introduce future tasks

Generating high levels of interaction in the classroom means going beyond simple instruction, breaking out of the vicious circle described opposite and overcoming what has been called 'the teacher's addiction to the right answer'.

Going beyond instruction

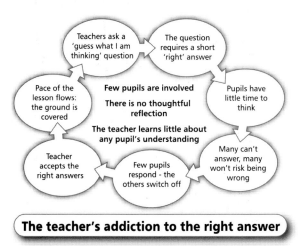

Teachers ask a 'guess what I am thinking' question

The question requires a short 'right' answer

Pace of the lesson flows: the ground is covered

Few pupils are involved

There is no thoughtful reflection

The teacher learns little about any pupil's understanding

Pupils have little time to think

Teacher accepts the right answers

Few pupils respond - the others switch off

Many can't answer, many won't risk being wrong

The teacher's addiction to the right answer

This section will examine how to break out of the vicious circle, allowing as many pupils as possible to communicate their understandings.

We can do this by:

- Asking better questions
- Asking questions better
- Devising activities that promote discussion

Ask more 'fat' or 'hot' questions

It has been estimated that in an average career a teacher will ask over a million questions, the vast majority of which they know the answer to!

Far too many of these are lower order questions which simply require factual recall. They are designed to get pupils to reproduce what they already know and to engage them in the lesson, but they do not require or produce thinking. These kinds of questions may keep pupils awake but they do not help them to learn anything new.

Teachers can improve students' learning by asking fewer but better questions. Better or 'higher order thinking' questions are sometimes called 'fat' or 'hot' questions. They:

- **Focus attention:**   *'What does this tell us about...?'*
- **Force comparisons:**   *'What is the same and what is different about...?'*
- **Seek clarification:**   *'How can we explain...?'*
- **Stimulate enquiry:**   *'What would happen if...?' 'What do we need to know?'*
- **Look for reasons:**   *'How can we be sure that...?' 'Why do you think that?'*

Open and closed questions

Good questions can be either 'open' or 'closed'. **Closed questions** have a single right answer; **open questions** have a number of possible answers.

Whether a question is open or closed may not lie in the question itself but in the teacher's reason for asking the question. *'What colour is the sky?'* might be a closed question in a science lesson and an open question in an art lesson, for instance.

Traditionally it has been thought that closed questions are bad and open questions are good. It's true that open questions often work better than closed ones. For example, *'Is 7 a prime number?'* might elicit responses like, *'Err…yes I think so'* or, *'No, it's not'.* This won't let you assess a pupil's understanding of the properties of prime numbers. Changing the question to *'Why is 7 an example of a prime number?'* forces pupils to think, and invites them to demonstrate that thinking.

But closed questions can be good too, especially when there is a misconception you want to reveal, eg: *'Is grass alive or dead?'*; *'Is it always true that metals are magnets?'*

'Hot' questions for incorrect answers

Incorrect answers present a valuable opportunity to use 'hot' questions to check and develop a pupil's understanding.

Don't just rush to a judgement or give the correct answer. Use a range of hot checking questions like the ones here:

What do you think?

How do you know?

Why do you think that?

Do you have a reason?

Can you be sure?

Is there another way?

The aim should be to correct the error by eliciting a better answer.

Give pupils 'think time'

Research has shown (see Mary Budd Rowe, page 124) that teachers leave very little time between asking the class a question and choosing a pupil to answer (often less than a second!). Yet to give considered responses to 'fat' questions, pupils need more thinking time.

Leave three to ten seconds 'think' or 'wait' time when asking fat questions. This acknowledges that thinking takes time. It also implies that the pupil, not the teacher, should be thinking.

Other advantages of think time are:
- It helps pupils to rephrase ideas in their heads
- More pupils are likely to be able to offer an answer
- Responses are usually more thoughtful and creative

Slowing the pace of classroom discussion is hard if you feel under pressure to cover content or you have a class with challenging behaviour. It's also hard for both teachers and pupils to get used to. Some teachers combine it with 'no hands up' (page 54).

Teachers need 'wait time' too

There are actually two kinds of think or wait time:

Two kinds of wait time

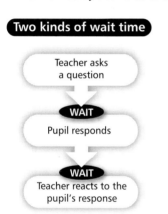

Teacher asks a question

WAIT

Pupil responds

WAIT

Teacher reacts to the pupil's response

As teachers we also tend to react to the pupil's response very quickly without giving ourselves time to interpret that response and consider how to respond.

We are particularly prone not to leave wait time after the pupil has responded when we are asking 'guess what I am thinking' questions. We tend to come in with quick evaluative responses such as:

'Yes', 'No', 'Right', 'Wrong' or
'Nearly', 'Almost', 'Not quite'...

Leaving more time after the pupil has responded allows us to use minimal encouragers (page 51) and/or do more reflective listening (page 52).

Minimal encouragers

Minimal encouragers help children to keep talking. They are brief responses used to indicate that you are still there, listening. They involve saying very little and offer minimal direction. They can be sprinkled throughout the conversation but they may be particularly useful at the beginning, where they can help to add momentum.

You might simply respond by not saying anything but raising your eyebrows or murmuring *'mmm…'*. It suggests: *'Please continue. I'm listening and I understand.'* There are many others worth using, for instance:

'Tell me more', 'Oh?', 'For instance?', 'I see', 'Right', 'Then?', 'Yes really?', 'And?', 'Go on', 'So?', 'I hear you', 'Sure'…

Minimal encouragers do not imply agreement or disagreement. *'Right'* means not that you agree but, *'Yes, I hear what you are saying. Go on.'*

Reflective listening

Teachers need to be reflective listeners. Reflective listeners restate the feeling and/or content of what a speaker has said in way that demonstrates understanding and acceptance. Reflective listening should be non-judgemental, accurate and concise. It involves paraphrasing the essence of what has been said and reflecting that back to the speaker, eg:

'So you think that...', *'You seem to be saying that...'*, *'It seems to me that you feel...'*

You can use paraphrasing to reflect children's emotions or understandings back to them. It is particularly good to use reflective listening before judging, arguing, criticising or trying to come up with a solution.

You need to use reflective listening at the right time. Don't use it when you can't be accepting because of the circumstances or when you are too pressured or hassled to really listen. Don't use it when the pupil can't think through the immediate problem and urgently needs help from you as an adult.

Take an answer round the class

Questioning in many classrooms is like table-tennis. The teacher pings a question to the class, picks a pupil to pong an answer back, then pings a reply back to them. Try playing volleyball instead and keep the game on the pupils' side of the net by taking the answer round the class.

If it is a closed question ask one pupil the question and ask another if the answer seems right. Then ask a third pupil for an explanation of why it seems so.

With open questions if a pupil gives an answer that needs improvement, don't suggest a change yourself. Instead, say, *'Wait there till we see what others think,'* and gather some answers or suggestions from other pupils. Make a point of bringing these answers back to the first pupil and ask, *'Which answer do you like best?'* or *'What do you think now?'*

This involves the rest of the class while still keeping the first pupil listening and thinking.

No hands up

'No hands up' involves the teacher departing from standard practice by not asking for hands up to answer. Unless specifically asked, pupils know *not* to put their hands up when the teacher asks a question. The teacher can call on anyone to answer and everyone is expected to be able to answer at any time, even if it is with, *'I don't know'*.

The no hands rule can completely change the dynamic in the classroom. It makes it difficult for pupils to switch off from class discussions. It's much more likely to work well when used with increasing wait time to help students think about their answers.

'No hands up' can be difficult for both teacher and pupils to get used to. If it proves too much of a change, an alternative is to continue with the standard routine of asking for hands up but if only one or two hands go up to start with, tell the class you are waiting for a few more before you ask someone to answer.

Think, pair and share

'Think, pair and share' is a well-used and effective technique for encouraging classroom participation and interaction.

First of all, pupils write down as many answers, ideas or suggestions as they can think of on their own (**Think**). Then they pool their ideas with a partner (**Pair**) and finally the teacher opens the discussion up for contributions from the class as a whole (**Share**).

This simple strategy helps all pupils to learn by encouraging a sustained interaction between thinking and talking, both individually and in groups.

You can make it as flexible and formal as you like. Some teachers enforce absolute silence during the 'think' stage and as soon as the class are asked to 'think, pair and share' they know they have one minute to write down their ideas without any talking.

Ask for five

A technique that helps to take account of different abilities is to 'ask for five'.

Ask pupils to write down five ideas, solutions, possibilities, suggestions, etc about the topic under discussion. After allowing an appropriate amount of time, different pupils can then be asked for just one idea each.

'Asking for five' stretches able children without exposing those who aren't able to think of five ideas. There is also the possibility that weaker pupils will be able to add to their own ideas as the lesson proceeds.

This idea can be combined with 'think, pair and share'.

Beat the teacher

'Beat the teacher' is a good way of stimulating open thinking as an alternative to closed questions and right/wrong answers.

Explain to the class that you are likely to make some mistakes in what you are about to do and that they should work individually to spot and note down as many mistakes as they can. Carry out your task and, at the end, ask pairs of pupils to compare their results and compile a joint list. Each pair can then offer a mistake for wider class discussion, developing and clarifying points, etc. Finally, everyone can write up the corrections they have discussed.

In languages work, for instance, the teacher can read a passage in the foreign language which contains mistakes like faulty pronunciation, incorrect syntax, mixed tenses, etc. The responsibility for diagnosing errors is placed on the pupils, not the teacher.

Suitable tasks include:

- Describing a procedure
- Reading a text
- Writing a passage on the board
- Demonstrating a practical activity
- Explaining a concept
- Working though a calculation
- Drawing a diagram on an overhead projector

Get on the carousel

Carousel brainstorming gets everyone working together in small groups to generate lots of ideas quickly. It is most effective when several ideas or kinds of ideas are being managed at once. For example, ideas for getting a hippo out of a bath could be organised into nasty ways, funny ways, expensive ways and kind ways.

Participants work in groups of three to five. Each group has a different coloured marker pen and writes down as many ideas as possible for three to five minutes. Then the groups move to the next station, leaving their list of ideas behind them and taking their pen with them to comment on and add new ideas to those already devised by the last group at that station. The carousel continues until every group has visited each station. Groups then return to their original station to review the list they find there.

A less energetic way of turning the carousel is to make the lists go round instead of the groups.

The jigsaw technique

A good way to remember what you have learned is to immediately use the learning to teach someone else. The 'jigsaw' technique is a useful tool for this. It is also a way to help pupils access a lot of information in a short time.

The content to be covered is divided up and each group is given something different to investigate or study.

For example, a class of 30 pupils is studying the Second World War. The teacher arranges the pupils into five groups of six and gives each group a different task. They have to research rationing, anti-Semitism, evacuation, the changing role of women and the home front. The groups work collaboratively to produce a report or a summary of their subject area.

Now comes the 'jigsaw'. Five groups of six reform into six groups of five (one representative from each area studied.) The pupils in their new groups take it in turn to share their summaries. Numbers in the jigsaw technique vary to suit group or class sizes.

Feedback is a two-way process

If there is one word that summarises most of what assessment for learning is about, it is **feedback**.

> **Feedback is a** **two-way process**

In this chapter we've looked at how we can get quality feedback from our pupils as they are learning. By 'tuning in' to what they say and finding out what and how they have learned, we become aware of our students' partial understandings or misunderstandings.

The following two chapters look at how to give feedback to pupils. First verbal feedback and then written feedback.

Assessment
and Learning

 Learning
Intentions and
Success Criteria

 Quality Interaction

 Verbal Feedback ◀

 Written Feedback

 Assessment
by Pupils

 Getting Started

 Further
Information

Verbal
Feedback

The lifeblood of learning

Feedback has been called the lifeblood of learning. If you ask pupils, no matter what their ability, what would most help them learn better the vast majority will say more immediate feedback from the teacher as they are learning.

Along with questioning and explaining, giving feedback is one of the basic tools of the teacher's trade. It allows teachers to help pupils bridge the gap between what they currently know and can do and what they are expected to know and do. (See page 17.)

Giving feedback is a highly developed skill that teachers hone over years in the job. We all know that vague praise or exhortations such as *'Your essay is good'* or *'You'll need to work harder at your spelling'* are no good unless they are followed by specific advice about why it is good or how to improve.

Finding time for oral feedback

Pupils may want more immediate verbal feedback but finding time for this is hard. You can use a range of strategies to maximise it:

- Conserve time wasted distributing materials by giving pupils direct access to resources: paper, spare pens/pencils, dictionaries, help sheets, etc
- Time desk activities to give you enough time for feedback but not so long that your pupils' interest flags
- Support pupils by providing access to sources of help other than yourself: checklists, reference books, prompt sheets, calculators, spell-checkers
- Establish routines to ration out your time fairly, for example having a list of steps on the wall to go through before calling on help from the teacher
- Manage your time so that, for instance, a third of the class gets quality oral feedback every third lesson

Despite measures such as these, the time you have is always going to be at a premium, so you need to use it as effectively as you can. That is mainly what this section is about.

Balancing two kinds of feedback

Experienced teachers know that good teaching means balancing and mixing the two kinds of feedback illustrated opposite. They are able to offer descriptions and opinions, give judgements and evaluations, while still accepting young people for who they are. They recognise that positive feedback opens ears and motivates and too much negative criticism deafens, so they accentuate the positive but don't eliminate the negative. They try their best to balance accuracy and approval, honest criticism and support.

They also learn to recognise that different children respond differently to different kinds of feedback on different occasions. They know what kind of feedback individual pupils or pairs want and also form views of what they need.

Balancing two kinds of feedback

Focus on the task, not the person

When giving feedback about a difficulty, don't discourage a pupil by focusing on the person more than the task. Comments like, *'You used to be good at this'* or *'You're not getting the hang of this, are you?'* give the impression that you don't think the pupil can master the task in hand.

On the other hand, comments like *'This seems to be causing you a bit of bother'* or *'This is difficult, isn't it?'* carry the message that the task itself is troublesome. Couple this with a helpful suggestion about a possible way of approaching the problem and you can offer the incentive and direction to deal with the difficulty.

Acknowledge young people's feelings

In the long run, accepting and respecting children's feelings can be more positive than trying to bully them out of their negative feelings with *'Of course you can do it'* or similar expressions.

Be prepared to listen with empathy. Avoid dismissing what children are saying or feeling, and give them the message that it is OK to have negative thoughts. Acknowledge their feelings with a sound or a word (*'Mmm, I see.'*) or with a sentence: *'I can see that you are disappointed.'* Identify with them: *'I know it can be upsetting when you get things wrong.'*

Focus on effort and technique

Recent research (see Carol Dweck page 124) suggests that many people in our society think their intelligence (whether for maths, language, music or art for instance) is fixed at birth. If this is the case, then no matter how bright they actually are they tend to give up when they can't do something because they don't think making an effort or using a different technique will make any difference.

If these people are criticised for being dim or even praised for being bright that can simply strengthen their belief that there is not much they can do about it.

On the other hand, focusing your feedback on the effort they are making or the strategies they are using can help to overcome or lessen their beliefs about ability being unchangeable and encourage them to withstand and even thrive on setbacks.

Keep comments positive and specific

Comments such as *'You need to be more detailed in your description of scientific experiments'* or *'You need to vary the sentence structure in your writing'* might inform pupils **what** they need to improve, but do not show them **how** to improve. Comments that help pupils to improve need to be more specific.

Some teachers keep their comments positive and specific by sandwiching what they think should be improved between two positive comments. The first positive comment can be about what's good in a piece of work. The improvement can come next to be followed with a helpful suggestion about how to make the improvement.

All three points should be specific, as in our example.

First positive comment

'Good work, John. I liked when you described the sun as a 'ball of fire' but you need to think more about what to say about the water. Try thinking about how it reflects things.'

Something that could be improved

Positive suggestion for how to make improvement

Make feedback reflect why you set the work

Feedback should articulate well with the learning intention and success criteria set at the start of an activity. This helps to ensure that the learning process is coherent for the learner. It also maintains the focus on improving learning.

For example, an appropriate learning intention in science could be, *'We are learning about how parachutes work'* and the associated success criteria might be, *'I'm looking for you to tell me what friction is and why it helps a parachute to let something fall safely from the sky.'*

After pupils have experimented with model parachutes and written up the results, feedback reflecting the purpose of the work set would refer to the learning intention and especially the success criteria by highlighting how well the results explained that when air and the parachute rub together, friction is produced to slow the fall.

'Well done. I can see you've discovered that contact between the air and the parachute makes it fall more slowly. Can you think of some more examples where a similar thing is happening?'

Avoid undeserved or excessive praise

When giving feedback, accentuating the positive is critically important, but beware the pitfalls of praise. The best teachers actually praise less than average. Handing out gold stars on every occasion and praising children for almost anything often does more harm than good. In extreme cases, it can lead to frustration and resentment.

To be valued, it needs to confirm a child's own sense of reality. Even young children are much more able than many adults appreciate to work out what 'doing well' means. If children are told from an early age that everything they do is wonderful or that they are geniuses, then they become confused and can't develop their own critical judgement.

Praise is often used as a trick to get children to change their behaviour. This is likely to be resented because it is correctly regarded as an attempt to manipulate and control. Rather than using praise in ways children perceive as dishonest, parents and teachers really need to help children to develop their own standards of performance.

Less praise, more encouragement

Part of the problem with praise is what's being praised: is it the person or what they've done? The person receiving the praise can have difficulty in telling the difference. If they believe that it's because of who they are and not what they've achieved, then it can make them complacent. Some of the common problems with praise can be overcome by focusing on encouragement:

- Praise often comes at the end of a task, while encouragement can be given at any time
- Students often have to earn praise, while encouragement can be given without having to be triggered in some way, or just for making an effort
- Praise often has the effect of making students put a priority on pleasing the teacher, while encouragement accepts them for being themselves
- Praise is often vague, while encouragement can be explicit and informative

Opinions or judgements?

As teachers we can be quick to rush to judgement, and of course making and giving judgements are necessary parts of the job. But a judgement can sometimes come too soon and can be taken as a final verdict, usually on some past effort.

Whereas praise frequently involves a judgement, offering an opinion expresses views that are personal and tend to be forward-looking. They involve making more 'I' statements than 'you' statements:

- *'I enjoyed reading your essay and I like the way you've laid it out'*
- *'I'm pleased with the progress you've made'*
- *'I'm disappointed with your report. I feel you haven't put as much work into it as usual. I know you can do better'*

If sincere, statements like this do not need the substantiation a judgement would. Instead of suggesting that someone is good or bad, they convey that the effort is valued and the risk the teacher is taking by sharing a personal response.

Appreciation – an alternative to praise

Showing your appreciation is another alternative to praise. If genuine, it is a fact rather than an evaluation. It demonstrates positive regard and involves taking a risk, sharing something of yourself.

Instead of praising, try showing your appreciation for who young people are and what they have done, eg:

Treat people the same by appreciating their differences

Praise can have different effects depending on how it is used and the disposition of the recipient. In general, praise is best used for what children can do, not who they are. Praise children for succeeding at things they can control but which cause them difficulty: praise badly behaved boys for behaving well but not quiet girls; praise quiet girls for speaking up but not loud-mouthed boys.

Used in this way, praise can perform a valuable function in providing the feedback that helps children to reflect on how to achieve improvements in their own actions or behaviour.

Be yourself

This section has concentrated on styles of feedback and ways to improve the quality of the verbal feedback you give to pupils. Don't use the advice here to completely change your style – be yourself and play to your strengths. But if you have a particularly strong preference for one of the styles outlined on page 67, look for the ideas in this section that may help you to achieve a better balance between the two.

The next section deals with written feedback, ie marking. You'll find much of the advice we've just covered in 'Verbal Feedback' can be carried over into reflecting on how you give written feedback to pupils.

Written
Feedback

Make your comments count

When teachers are asked what they hate most about marking they usually talk about the time involved and how repetitive and boring it can be. You don't need to probe for long, however, to come up with the real reason they dislike marking:

So much of it has so little impact.

You spend a huge amount of time writing comments and suggestions for improvement and they just seem to be ignored; the next piece of work comes back with exactly the same problems.

Even if they couldn't reduce the time they spend marking, most teachers would be happy putting the same amount of time into marking if only they got more back from it.

The following pages look at how to make marking manageable and how to make your comments count. They begin by exploring how by marking less you can actually achieve more.

Some things don't work

For years teachers have been taking bagloads of jotters home and covering them dutifully with red pen. As a teacher of English once said to me, *'We are martyrs to our marking – we are addicted to it.'*

Copy-edit marking is where you mark every detail (eg punctuation, spellings, etc.) as well as the content. It is very time-consuming and has less impact than people think. There is simply too much for pupils to respond to and it can demoralise them.

Vague comments and exhortations are less time-consuming than copy-edit marking but just as ineffective. They include general summary comments at the end of a piece of work and short, personal, emotionally-based comments in the margin on what you thought was good or bad. They generally evaluate but don't prescribe what or how things could be improved.

Mark according to success criteria

The best strategy for making marking manageable for both you and your pupils is to resist the temptation (and the pressure) to mark everything in every piece of work.

Instead, focus in on the agreed success criteria for that piece of work and mark only to these criteria. It means that in a piece of writing, for instance, you will sometimes focus on grammar and at other times you will focus on aspects of content.

Given that this is a radical departure from common practice in many schools, an individual teacher may not have the power to make this change. It may require a change of policy.

But what about spelling?

Spelling is a contentious issue. Teachers of all subjects often feel a great temptation to correct spelling when marking. Some schools oblige them to. However, it can be better to deal with spelling problems in a different context from normal marking activities. A compromise may be the best way, with subject teachers in secondary, for example, focusing on the spelling of specific technical terms.

A primary teacher was never fully convinced that she could ignore routine errors like the identification of new sentences and mis-spelling of familiar words. She uses (sparingly) a set of eyes in the left margin looking sideways towards the pupil's work, signifying 'oops'. The error can be further indicated or not. It's non-threatening, even attractive and the eyes are easily and quickly drawn by the teacher.

Use 'highlight and prompt' marking

A marking strategy that enables you to mark to the success criteria agreed with the pupils for each piece of work is **'highlight and prompt'** marking.

You highlight (with a highlighter pen) 'growth points', ie two or three aspects of the work that have been successful in terms of the learning intentions and success criteria. You then identify one area for improvement, link it with an arrow to the nearest white-space and write a prompt to help the child make a small improvement.

'Highlight and prompt' is popular because it doesn't involve marking everything in every piece of work and it makes the task of following up on the marking more manageable for pupils. It's also known as:

- Bubbles and boxes (page 90)
- Growth points and next steps
- Two stars and a wish
- Pink and green

Highlight the positives

Highlighting does not exclude you from writing positive general comments such as, *'Lovely sentence to start your story'*, but using a highlighter pen is quick and easy. You can indicate small successes and make them instantly obvious to pupils.

In English you might highlight the use of similes in a descriptive piece of writing because this was the focus for the lesson; if the writing was personal you might highlight descriptions of feelings.

Pupils can do this for themselves as well or they can peer-assess in the same manner. It's a good way of encouraging self-assessment and making pupils more responsible for their own learning.

'Close the gap' prompts

Pupils need to know not only what they need to improve but how to achieve the improvement. It is writing the prompt that merits your time. Your prompt should help pupils to close the gap between where they are now and where they want to get to in terms of a particular learning goal.

The best kind of prompt is one that gives just enough help to point learners in the right direction. Too little help won't achieve this and can have a negative effect on pupil motivation; too much help can mean the goal is reached with no extra effort. Try using:

- Reminder prompts (page 87)
- Scaffolding prompts (page 88)
- Example prompts (page 89)

Reminder prompts

Reminder prompts simply ask for more detail or elaboration without giving any further help. They don't take up much of the teacher's time and work well with able children, who can work independently.

- *'Tell me more about photosynthesis'*
- *'Give more detail'*
- *'Write a more interesting end to this story'*
- *'Your solutions are all correct, but a bit brief'*
- *'Re-do this multiplication problem'*
- *'You need to present your graphs more clearly'*
- *'Explain why you think this'*

The trouble is that many teachers write this kind of prompt for all children and most need more support than this. They need scaffolding and example prompts.

Scaffolding prompts

Scaffolding prompts provide a learning framework for children who need more support than a simple reminder. They give specific advice about how to improve the original answer, helping students to extend their present understanding and develop more complex answers:

- *'Tell me more about photosynthesis: what is needed? How does...? When exactly did...?'*
- *'Give more detail about the importance of....for instance...'*
- *'Write a more interesting end to the story. You might consider...'*
- *'Re-do this problem. You could try...'*
- *'You seem to be confusing sine and cosine. Can you work out the difference?'*
- *'You need to present your graphs more clearly so that the reader can see...'*

Example prompts

Example prompts can be extremely successful with all children, but especially with average or below average children. They take longer to write because they make suggestions, offer information or even give the pupil a choice of actual words or phrases:

- *'Try to describe the setting, eg: the house was dark when we went inside, and very quiet. Outside, the sun was shining so…'*

- *'It might be interesting to know what Shannon did when she touched the ground. Did she look around or hunt for mum and dad?'*

- *'Choose one of these or your own: 'He is a good friend because he never says unkind things about me.' 'My friend is a friend because he never tells me lies.'*

- *'Look at the multiplication table and highlight the facts you know very well and find ways of working out the ones you don't know so well, eg what facts would help you work out 7x8?'*

Make prompts accessible and visible

Making your prompts accessible and visible helps all learners but especially younger and less able learners.

A primary teacher took a digital photograph of each child. She cut it out and stuck it landscape on to a sheet of A4 coloured card. She drew a big bubble cloud and a box on the card, decorated it with stars, glitter etc and laminated it.

Each child has their card beside them showing something they are doing well and the next step, target or prompt written on in whiteboard marker pen so that it can be changed and updated at any time.

Provide time and incentives for response

There is obviously not much point in spending a lot of time writing comments and prompts if you don't give pupils time in class or incentives to spend their own time responding to them.

One way to do this is to ask pupils to number all the pages in their jotters. Have them construct two columns on the inside cover, one for you and one for them. Once you have marked a piece of work, note down the page numbers and the date in your column and sign it. Pupils should do the same in the opposite column once they have done the follow-up work required. You do not mark the next piece of work until they've followed up and filled in their column. If parents complain, you explain why and have the evidence to support your position.

Two-thirds-of-the-way tests

Marking end-of-topic tests comes too late for pupils to do anything to correct misunderstandings that have arisen during the topic. You could, however, set a two-thirds-of-the-way through-topic test to identify any learning needs and allow time to address them.

You could, like one secondary Maths department, combine this with a traffic lights activity. All the pupils look through their tests and think about where and why they have made mistakes. They use the traffic lights code to record their understanding of aspects of the topic. If they have done well in part of the test and feel confident about it, they put a green blob on a record of attainment designed for the purpose. If they have done well but think it was a fluke, they put an amber blob. They might have made only silly mistakes they know won't happen again and therefore put a green blob. If poor answers were because they didn't understand a part of the topic, then they would use a red blob.

When gathered together, the records of attainment can be used to identify what needs to be covered again in some way, either with the whole class or in smaller groups working on clearing up a shared misunderstanding.

To grade or not to grade?

To be effective your written comments need to cause thinking and give pupils help to improve. We all know that grades or marks on their own don't do that and vague comments like *'Good work'* don't do that.

However, a large body of research uncovered by Black and Wiliam (see page 12) suggests that giving both a mark and a comment, no matter how insightful and helpful the comment, does not generally lead to improvement either. This is the most controversial of their findings.

Giving both a mark and a comment is the most common way of marking in the UK. Teachers are programmed to give marks and pupils are programmed to receive them. This is also what parents expect, and everyone from the prime minister downwards is at pains to tell us that pupils need to know where they stand. But the research is clear:

> The only written feedback that leads reliably to improvement is where you give a comment only and leave off a mark or a grade.

Retiring hurt

Let's focus for a moment on why grading work can be counterproductive. Paul Black borrowed the phrase 'retiring hurt' from cricket to describe the psychology:

"When the classroom focuses on rewards, 'gold stars' or 'place-in-the-class' ranking, then pupils look for ways to obtain the best marks, rather than to become better learners. Or they simply seek to 'get by' and avoid difficult tasks. Or even worse, they simply give up and 'retire hurt'."

Black and Wiliam, *'Inside the Black Box'.*

Pupils who receive a good mark ignore the comments because they don't think they need to do better; those who receive a poor mark don't read the comments because they are upset. Pupils who want to improve, and believe that they can, will read the comments, but under-confident pupils, no matter what their ability, will not act on them.

| A belief that ability is fixed | ➕ | Assessment designed to measure and compare | ➤ | Many pupils retiring hurt |
| A belief that all can achieve | ➕ | Assessment designed to provide feedback on how to improve | ➤ | Increased resilience and self-confidence |

Don't put a mark on every piece of work

Most teachers recognise that grading can have a negative effect on many pupils but it is also true that many pupils and their parents expect grades or marks out of ten on every piece of work, indeed many are 'hooked' on them!

Black and Wiliam did not suggest that teachers should never grade children's work. That would be neither practical nor desirable. Pupils need to know where they stand but the question is: how regularly do they need to know where they stand?

Black and Wiliam suggested the best strategy is to give marks as seldom as possible while children are learning and to use only comments to help direct future efforts. In primary and lower secondary you might want to issue a mark once a term in each aspect of their work. As pupils get nearer national examinations they will need to know how well they are doing more regularly.

Plus, minus or equals

If the research is telling us that giving grades can mean that able pupils become complacent if their grades are always good, why not try something different? Challenge your most able pupils by not giving them a traditional grade for a piece of work; give them instead a plus, minus or equals, depending on how it compares with the last piece of work they did.

This can work for all students, but bright ones who want to cruise hate it!!

Respect pupils' work

However we mark pupils' work, it's worth remembering that they feel that their efforts are defaced by scribbled comments they cannot make sense of. So, when marking a piece of work, don't deface it with a lot of scores, ticks, crosses, question or exclamation marks. Try not to use too much red ink, either.

You can show pupils you think their work is more valuable than that by minimising the disfiguring effects of marking. For example, you can use:

* Post-it® notes
* Wrap-around sheets
* Comments neatly written in the margins
* Discreet codes and shared marking conventions
* Neat underlines and circles

Try to keep marking on the work itself to the minimum you need to get the message across. You might also use pencil, which can be rubbed out later when any suggestions have been dealt with.

Stepping stones to responsibility

Getting pupils to take more responsibility for their own learning doesn't just happen. It grows out of the kinds of strategies in this book, namely:

- Pupils knowing what they are expected to learn and how they will know they have been successful
- Teachers creating a climate in the classroom where there is open and honest dialogue about learning
- Teachers modelling the giving and receiving of quality feedback
- Teachers putting more emphasis on improvement and less on performance

The next chapter looks at how to build on these stepping stones to promote pupils' self- and peer-assessment.

Assessment
and Learning

 Learning
Intentions and
Success Criteria

 Quality Interaction

 Verbal Feedback

 Written Feedback

 Assessment
by Pupils ◀

 Getting Started

 Further
Information

Assessment
by Pupils

Let go so they can get going

> **Assessment by pupils, far from being a luxury, is an essential part of formative assessment.**
>
> Paul Black and Dylan Wiliam

There are two fundamentally good reasons for promoting and developing self- and peer-assessment.

The first is purely pragmatic. If immediate good quality verbal feedback tailored to your specific needs is so important in learning and a secondary teacher has 30 pupils in a class for, say, 60 minutes at a time and all the feedback has to come from and through the teacher, pupils will never get enough.

Secondly, and even more importantly, one of the basic premises on which assessment for learning is built is the need to help learners to take more responsibility for their own learning.

It's OK to make mistakes

If there is one essential factor for promoting assessment by pupils, it is that a climate is established where pupils **of all abilities** believe the following and behave as if they do:

- It's OK to make mistakes
- There's no need to conceal your difficulties
- It's OK to be stuck
- It's normal and acceptable to get something wrong

It's about establishing relationships and about focusing on the language in the classroom. This is not easy; it's something that needs the constant attention of the teacher.

Three strategies

This chapter contains three practical strategies for promoting assessment by pupils:

1. Modelling good quality products and processes (pages 103 – 104).
2. Working more effectively in pairs (pages 106 – 108).
3. Reflecting on how you learn (pages 109 – 117).

Many teachers suggest that you cannot employ some of these strategies until pupils are trustworthy, but experience shows that introducing the strategies carefully and with support can help pupils to become trustworthy and to take responsibility for their own learning.

A nose for quality

Providing lists of success criteria for what makes a good piece of work, a good product or good performance is not, on its own, enough to help pupils progress and improve. You need to talk about quality all the time.

Use success criteria regularly to look at products and performances and ask, *'What makes them good?'*

For example, what makes a good:

- Discussion?
- Diagram?
- Poster?
- Essay?

- Corner kick?
- Drum roll?
- Muffin?
- Argument?

- Story?
- Friendship?
- Experiment?
- Report?

The list goes on and spreads to every corner of the curriculum.

Generating success criteria with pupils (page 33) takes you into these kinds of discussions.

Model good work

Teachers commonly spend time marking or discussing pieces of work with the whole class. You can project the piece of work on a screen or make a photocopy for each member of the class.

It can be an anonymous piece of work from a pupil not in the class or it could be a member of the class's work used with the permission of the pupil responsible for it. A published work or a well-known masterpiece can be used as an alternative.

You can help a group to see more clearly how specific learning intentions and success criteria are used to evaluate a piece of work. It can help pupils understand your way of marking and support them to work on their own self-assessment skills.

Displays of work can be mounted on classroom walls or in corridors with the criterion-related features that have made a difference highlighted:
'This is good because …'

Learning together

We learn through having conversations – with ourselves inside our heads and with other people. Research suggests that conversations with other people are very important.

Black and Harrison et al (see page 124) found that if they haven't understood something after a second explanation from a teacher, boys don't ask again because they don't want to be seen as stupid. Girls don't ask again because they don't want to waste the teacher's time. But when they are peer assessing they will go on asking each other.

The evidence is that where the conditions are right, pupils who work together do not only receive more feedback and support, they can also get better quality feedback and support than they might get from a teacher. This is not just because they will go on asking each other if they do not understand, but because pupils often use language which is more accessible and understandable to each other than that of a teacher.

The challenge for the teacher is getting the conditions right for this to happen.

It's not just about sitting in pairs

Walk into most classrooms and you will see pupils sitting and working in pairs. The crucial question is: are they learning in pairs?

Paired working can be used more formally and more systematically for a range of purposes, eg:

- Marking or commenting on each other's work
- Teaching other pupils aspects of the topic
- Helping each other to revise for a test

Consider using the term 'learning partners' to emphasise the nature of the pairing. Other commonly used terminology includes 'response partners', 'marking partners', 'talk partners' or 'learning buddies'. Choose a term that both you and your pupils are comfortable with and understand. But if you do want to make more systematic, more formal and more varied use of paired working, it's a good idea to emphasise **learning** rather than talking or marking and to emphasise **working partnerships** rather than friendships.

Choosing learning partners

'I enjoy working with partners but not with friends. They don't tell you the truth. It needs to be someone who will be honest with you and help you improve.'

Upper primary school pupil.

Learning partners are best chosen by the teacher and they ought not to be based on friendships. In a class that is set it might be best to partner pupils randomly, with some consideration of social factors. In mixed ability classes aim to ensure that there is not too great an ability gap between the partners, but like all rules there are exceptions and sometimes pupils with a wide ability gap can work well together.

There are strong arguments for moving pairs around every five weeks or so. Pupils get used to working with people they do not easily get on with and in classes where there are one or more pupils who are difficult to work with, it means they are shared around. You can be open about this and explain how in the real world you need to be able to work with lots of different people, some of whom you get on with better than others.

Some ground rules

Learning partners need to be clear about what their role is and the ground rules for working together.

A pupil-friendly description of the role could be displayed on the wall, as a constant reminder of what a learning partner does.

For instance:

> *'A learning partner is someone who tells me the truth about my work and helps me make it better.'*

Ground rules on interaction can be generated with the pupils and again displayed prominently on the wall. How detailed the ground rules are will depend on the age of the learners and their familiarity with this way of working. The rules should be designed to encourage dialogue rather than each pupil taking turns to be the teacher.

Help them learn to learn

Ultimately you want students to go beyond reflecting on what they have done and how they have done to thinking about what they have learned from doing it.

Learning to learn, developing the ability to stand back and reflect on your own learning (or **metacognition** to give it a fancy title) is the holy grail. It is what helps us transfer our learning to different situations. It is what helps us become more intelligent.

Encourage reflection on how they're learning

You can promote reflection about learning by talking with pupils about the strategies they use when they don't know the meaning of a word or can't do a sum. This not only helps them to become more conscious of what works for them, it also emphasises the point that if you use strategies, you can become 'unstuck'.

Questions to ask before learning:
'How am I going to do it?'
'Is it similar to anything I have done before?'
'Is it 'one of those'?'

Questions to ask during learning:
'Do I understand it so far?'
'Do I need to ask a question?'
'Am I on the right track?'
'Am I still on track?'
'Is there a different way?'

If children get into the habit of asking themselves these questions from an early age, by the time they reach the later stages of secondary school they will be much more self-reliant and capable learners.

Ask questions to promote reflection while learning

A primary teacher tried a new approach to teaching PE by involving pupils in games such as football, hockey, rugby and so on and then stopping them every so often to ask them questions:

'How can you pass the ball successfully to another player?'
'What did you do that enabled you to receive the ball more easily?'
'What is the effect on the defender if your team passes firmly, accurately and early?'

These questions challenged pupils to think more carefully about the game and how they were playing it and led to huge improvements in their standards of play. It has also helped her to give coaching advice while they play. For instance, *'Look for your passing lane'* has become a common feature of her dialogue during a coaching lesson.

Hold regular debriefing sessions

Regularly involve the class in discussion about the successes and difficulties they have experienced while working on a task. This kind of debriefing will give children insights into what helps them to learn and build their self-esteem. They will also be reassured to know that everyone finds learning difficult at times.

Use a wide range of self-evaluation questions during these sessions. Vary the questions, using three different ones each week so that it doesn't become boring or routine:

The most important thing I learned was...	*What I was most pleased about was....*
What I found difficult was.....	*What I have learned that is new is....*
What I found interesting was....	*What helped me when something got tricky was...*
What I enjoyed most was.....	
What I want to find out more about is....	*What really made me think was.....*
What I need more help with is....	*Right now I feel......*
What still puzzles me is.....	*I might have learned better if.....*
What surprised me was....	

Careful with wording

If pupils are to be more up-front about their failures and successes, the questions you use to stimulate self-evaluation need to be thoughtfully worded. If you simply ask *'Who found it easy?'* you are likely to get a competitive show of hands that may not reflect reality. If you ask *'What did you find easy about matching the pictures to the labels?'* you will redirect children's attention on to thinking about how they tackled the task. Other questions you might use to help pupils to talk more freely about their own learning are:

- *'How would you do things differently next time, knowing what you know now?'*
- *'What can you do now that you couldn't do before?'*
- *'How do you think we can use what we have learned today and in the future?'*

Instead of asking *'What did you find difficult?'* try questions like:

- *'What do we need to work more on?'*
- *'How could you help yourself?'*
- *'What could you do to help yourself understand?'*

Ask what you learned in school today

You can give students practice in assessing their own learning by making a habit yourself of asking them to reflect on what they have learned at the end of a lesson or the day. By making it the normal way for a lesson or the day to end, then it will become second nature and part of the routine. This can be done in different ways:

- Ask pupils to think of one thing they have learned today and get a few to share what that was
- Allow two minutes for silent reflection without asking anyone to share their thoughts
- Ask pupils to write down three things that they have learned on a piece of paper
- Ask pupils to spend 30 seconds telling their partner what they have learned
- Stand by the door and ask a random selection of children as they go out what they have learned

Learning logs or journals

Learning logs or journals let students keep notes of their thoughts and feelings about their work. A log need be no more than a ring binder and sheets of paper.

Some schools have developed Maths journals where children record how they've tackled problems and what they can do. These journals allow pupils to reflect on their learning and give teachers a very clear picture of how they're doing.

A log should belong to the pupil and they should have time in class to complete it. This will help pupils take it seriously and commit to using it. The teacher should have access to it to gather valuable information for progress reports, etc.

A typical log might ask pupils to complete at least three sentences from the list of statements used in debriefing (page 112).

Traffic lights for tests and exams

Another simple but powerful way of children signalling how they perceive their own learning again uses the 'traffic lights' idea (pages 55 and 92), this time to plan revision by evaluating strengths and weaknesses.

Pupils use 'traffic lights' to assess a list of key words or topics on which the test will be set. By doing this, they can identify the areas where they feel their learning is secure, which they mark in green, and where they need to concentrate their efforts, which they mark in amber or red.

These traffic lights then form the basis of a revision plan. Pupils can identify questions in past examination papers that test their red (and amber) areas, and use personal and group revision time to help them cover the topics where they are weakest.

Traffic light trays

A middle primary teacher worked a variation of traffic lights by having three trays coloured red, amber and green. Pupils were asked to put their work into the tray that best described how well they felt they had understood what had been taught. He usually used the trays for literacy and numeracy and the pupils were told at the start of the lesson that they would be traffic-lighting their work.

He found the pupils were honest about which tray they put their work into and that there was always a spread of jotters in each tray. It was an easy strategy to implement and as pupils came to understand the purpose of the trays it really ran itself. He also found that it made the marking easier in that the pupils had organised it for him.

Marking less and achieving more is possible

Many teachers, quite understandably, have had strong doubts about the idea that they could mark less and achieve more. The last two examples on pages 116 and 117 do exemplify how this is possible if you can get pupils to take more responsibility for their own assessment and their own learning.

One of the most consistent bits of feedback we have had from teachers who have employed the techniques in this book is how surprised they are at how insightful and helpful pupils of all abilities can be about how to improve their own and each other's learning.

They testify to the fact that, if we let go and provide the right kind of encouragement and support, young people can become less dependent. When we let go, they get going.

Assessment
and Learning

 Learning
Intentions and
Success Criteria

 Quality Interaction

 Verbal Feedback

 Written Feedback

 Assessment
by Pupils

 Getting Started ◀

 Further
Information

Getting Started

What will work for you?

A lot of what good teaching is about is encapsulated in this Pocketbook. Given what we now know about how people learn, it is clear that teaching must go beyond instruction. Explaining clearly, asking questions, encouraging dialogue and giving feedback are the essence of good teaching.

Whether you are a beginner or someone with many years of experience, there will be lots of affirmations in these pages for you – things you do and do well. But there will also be challenges – things you don't do or don't do as well as you would like to. Don't feel guilty about that. See these as opportunities for learning.

Don't dismiss an idea outright because it is not age- or subject-specific. Many of the ideas here have been used across subjects and key stages, sometimes with and sometimes without adaptation.

You are the professional – you'll decide which ideas in this book will work for you to develop your practice. The advice on the next three pages might guide you in your selection and help you plan how to introduce new ideas to your class.

The 4Ps – practical and personal

Try applying the '4Ps Rule' to any new idea:

Practical   **P**ersonal   **P**upils   **P**ersevere

Let's start with the first two – 'practical' and 'personal'. You must believe that you can make the idea work for **you** in **your classroom**, with **your class** taking into account how old your learners are, what you are teaching them, the relationship you have with them and they have with each other. Additionally, there are day-to-day frustrations and restrictions to consider, such as the size of the classroom, the amount of time available, and the interruptions that are part of every teacher's working day.

In my experience some teachers use these as 'get-out' clauses, saying in effect something like, *'I could never do that with my class, they can't be trusted'*. But it's my strong belief that you can use these ideas to **build relationships** and **establish trust**.

The 4Ps – pupils

My third 'P' is for 'pupils'. This for me is the most important one. If you are going to try a new idea out with an existing class, don't simply tell them what you are going to do differently, talk to them about why. There will only ever be one reason for using any of the ideas in this book – to help them learn better. Share this with your pupils like a teacher on one of our courses did.

She went back to her class determined to try 'wait time' (page 49). She told them she had been at an in-service training session learning new things and had learned something that *'might work for us'*.

She explained how every time she asked her class a question there were generally only two hands up – the same two hands, two girls. She would like more people to answer but realised she wasn't giving them a chance.

The 4Ps – persevere

She went on to explain how she would work wait time. She would use it only for 'fat' questions (page 46). She would flag a question up as a fat question before she asked it, then ask the question and count to five, then they could put their hands up.

The story she wanted to tell was of the first time she tried it with the class. She was counting to five and at the count of four a boy (who had never put his hand up in the class before) raised his hand. *'Great it's working already,'* she thought and called on him to respond. The boy replied, *'Miss I've forgotten the question!'*

This brings me to my last 'P' – 'persevere'. Some ideas work right away, but others don't – they need bedding down as both you and your pupils become used to them. And if just one or two of them can help pupils take more responsibility for their own learning and help you to work smarter rather than harder, how good would that be?

Further reading

Assessment for Learning: Putting it into Practice
Paul Black, Christine Harrison, Clare Lee, Bethan Marshall and Dylan Wiliam
Published by Open University Press, 2003

Formative Assessment in Action
Shirley Clarke
Published by Hodder Arnold, 2005

Inside the Black Box: Raising Standards Through Classroom Assessment
Paul Black and Dylan Wiliam
Published by nfer Nelson Publishing, 1998

Self Theories: Their Role in Motivation, Personality and Development
Carol S Dweck
Published by Psychology Press, Philadelphia, 1999

Wait-time and Rewards as Instructional Variables, their Influence in Language, Logic and Fate Control
Mary Budd Rowe
Paper presented at National Association for Research in Science Teaching, Chicago, Illinois, 1972

Websites and resources

Learning Unlimited	www.learningunlimited.co.uk
Department for Education and Skills	www.dfes.gov.uk/ISA
The Assessment Reform Group	www.assessment-reform-group.org
Qualifications and Curriculum Authority	www.qca.org.uk/7659.html
Learning and Teaching Scotland	www.ltscotland.org.uk/assess

Assessment for Learning: The Learning Set: five packs of materials for trainers
Learning Unlimited

About the author

Ian Smith

Ian is one of Scotland's foremost teacher educators. He founded Learning Unlimited, recently dubbed *'Scotland's most successful teacher development agency'* by the Times Educational Supplement, Scotland.

Ian has worked in Scottish education for more than 30 years as a secondary teacher and in various posts at national level. In 1996 while at the Scottish Consultative Committee on the Curriculum (SCCC) he wrote a paper entitled ***Teaching for Effective Learning***, which is credited with having a major influence on learning and teaching in Scotland. He is the principal author of a set of training materials on assessment for learning which have been taken up by more than half the schools in Scotland.

Ian is best known for running interactive seminars and workshops with large groups of teachers on a range of aspects of learning and teaching. In the past 12 years he has worked with over 40,000 of Scotland's teachers face-to-face – almost one in three of the entire profession. He has worked on assessment for learning with teachers in the United States and Hong Kong. He can be contacted at www.learningunlimited.co.uk

ACCELERATED
LEARNING
Pocketbook

A pocketful of tips, tools
and techniques to help you
students reach their potential

Brin Best

LEARNING
TO LEARN
Pocketbook

A pocketful of strategies
and study skills for
motivating learners to
register, retain, recall and
revise with confidence
and success

Tom Barwood

DYSLEXIA
Pocketbook

A pocketful of tips,
tools and techniques
to unlock the
potential of learners
with dyslexia

Julie Bennett

CREATIVE
TEACHING
Pocketbook

A pocketful of imagination,
inspiration and innovation to
help you become an even
more creative teacher

Roy Watson-Davis

Other titles from the Teachers' Pocketbooks Series

Order Form

Your details

Name _____

Position _____

School _____

Address _____

_____

_____

Telephone _____

Fax _____

E-mail _____

VAT No. (EC only) _____

Your Order Ref _____

Please send me:

		No. copies
Assessment & Learning _____	Pocketbook	☐
_____	Pocketbook	☐
_____	Pocketbook	☐
_____	Pocketbook	☐
_____	Pocketbook	☐

Order by Post

Teachers' Pocketbooks

Laurel House, Station Approach
Alresford, Hants. SO24 9JH UK

Order by Phone, Fax or Internet

Telephone: +44 (0)1962 735573
Facsimile: +44 (0)1962 733637
E-mail: sales@teacherspocketbooks.co.uk
Web: www.teacherspocketbooks.co.uk